Easy Stuff to make with Fluff!

GILLIAN HARRIS

PAVILION

*Dedicated to all The Fluff-a-tiers at
The Gilliangladrag Fluff-a-torium,
past and present*

Contents

What is *Fluff*?

I have used WOOLTOPS for most of the projects in this book. Wooltops are essentially pieces of 'unspun' wool that has been processed into long fluffy lengths.

This is the stuff that is used when yarn is spun, and it's also the stuff used in felting, both for wet felting and needle felting. It is light and woolly and fluffy, especially when it's new, so that's why I refer to it as 'fluff'! It's almost a cross between cotton wool and candyfloss!

When a sheep is shorn, the wool gets carefully washed, and then carded (brushed) and finally wound into a continuous length where all the fibres face the same direction. This is wooltops. It is often referred to as 'roving' as well – especially in the USA. It is usually sold by weight.

Any wooltops can be used for these projects, but the wool I like to use the most is Merino, as it's particularly fine, soft and fluffy – great for felting and spinning – and gets dyed into so many different colours. There's a terrific inspirational palette of colours to work with if you choose Merino!

I have also used a selection of other fibres and yarns in some of the projects, which start life as fluffy wooltops, but have been processed, spun and plied into different sorts of yarns.

AND WHERE DO I GET IT?

Wooltops 'fluff' can be found in yarn and wool shops, like my shop The Gilliangladrag Fluff-a-torium in Dorking, Surrey, UK. It can also be found on my website www.gilliangladrag.co.uk where we stock (and ship worldwide) over 60 different Merino wooltops colours, mixed packs and blends, plus wooltops from other sheep breeds as well.

Wooltops are sold by weight, usually in 100g (3½oz) bags, or in smaller amounts in mixed packs, or blends of more than one colour that have been carded together. It is usually less expensive than spun yarn, as you're not paying for the spinning part of the process when you buy it!

HOW MUCH SHOULD I GET?

Have a quick flick through the book and see which projects take your fancy. Some use a lot more 'fluff' than others! When you buy it, it often seems like a lot, but remember it is quite 'puffy' and full of air. When you squish it down and remove the air, you can see the real amount of wool.

Some projects (like paper plate weaving or wooltops pompoms) won't need much at all, whereas other bigger felting projects might need quite a bit more. Refer to the 'What you'll need' amounts in each project to give you an idea of how much to buy.

HOW SHOULD I STORE IT?

Newly processed wooltops are deliciously soft and fluffy and extra easy to use, but as time goes by the wool will attract moisture from the air and you'll notice the fluffy wooltops becoming a little more matted – or slightly felted – particularly if they are kept in a damp atmosphere. To prevent this from happening, try to store them in airtight containers or sealed bags. That way they will last for ages!

If you do end up with slightly matted wooltops, try 'teasing' them apart a little to make them fluffy again before using.

WHAT ABOUT USING OTHER FIBRES?

There are many other sorts of wool fibres and yarns out there that you can use. There are even 'man-made' fake wooltops fibres made from acrylic and nylon, but often only available in white. Be careful with these though – they are fine for some of the projects in the book (including needle felting), but they are no good for wet felting alone. Most other fibres work best when mixed in with your wooltops, rather than using them on their own, unless the project specifically calls for that.

Angelina Fabulous glittery strands that can be included in a lot of projects. You can also buy wooltops with them already included.

Silk Adds a sheen to your fluffy makes if it's mixed with the wool. Some wooltops are blended with it already too.

Curly wool locks Gorgeous little curly bits of wool from very curly sheep – great for adding interest and effects.

Yarns Too many and varied to mention! The list is endless; all the colours of the rainbow and fine lacy weights through to thick and chunky.

A NOTE ABOUT COLOURS

When specific wooltops are used in projects, the shade name is given – for example, Lettuce Green, Candy Pink. These colours can be found on the gilliangladrag website, or why not dye your own following the instructions on page 76?

Make Stuff

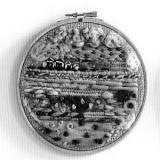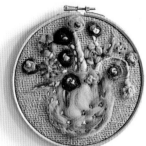

with Fluff!

LEVEL
EASY PEASY

Wooltops Pompoms

Make yourself the FLUFFIEST and EASIEST pompoms in the world, using fluffy unspun wool aka wooltops!

WHAT YOU'LL NEED

For one 10cm (4in) pompom

• Pompom maker, 9–10cm (3½–4in)

• 25g (1oz) or 1m (1yd) of your favourite wooltops colour or blend. Try mixing different colours together for more effects!

• Sharp scissors

• 20cm (8in) string or ribbon

HOW TO MAKE

1. Open up your pompom maker and get it ready for use. Split the wooltops in half lengthways and wrap half around the left side of the pompom maker and half around the right side, tucking in the ends. It's very fluffy and bulky but keep it as tight as you can.

2. Shut the pompom maker (and secure if it has clips to hold it together) and then start to snip all the way around with the sharp scissors. As you do this, the pompom will magically come to life!

3. Next it's very important to secure your new fluffy wooltops pompom with some strong string or ribbon, and tie it REALLY REALLY tightly. Leave some extra to hang.

4. Very carefully unclip the pompom maker and release your new fabulous fluffy pompom.

5. It might look a little bit straggly and messy when you first release it, so the last (and best) step is to give it a trim with your sharp scissors. Keep turning it while you cut it into a nice round shape and get rid of bits sticking out where they shouldn't be! Then it's ready to hang!

TOP TIP

If your fluffy wooltops pompoms look a little tired or become matted over time, simply retrim to give them a new lease of life!

Statement Fluff

Say what you mean and add words or letters to your wall or mantelpiece covered with pretty wools and yarns to match your décor. Make a statement!

WHAT YOU'LL NEED

• Wooden or metal letters

• Small amounts of wooltops and yarns in different colours

• Some strong glue suitable for use with wool

• Sticky tape

• Optional: wooltops pompoms to hang and decorate (see page 8)

HOW TO MAKE

1. Decide whether you are going to cover the whole of your letter or just part of it. As some of my larger letters were painted pretty colours, I decided just to use some wooltops outlined with a contrasting yarn on those ones.

2. Carefully place and wind around small amounts of wool and secure with the glue at the back. It's helpful to use a little sticky tape to hold the wool in place while it dries.

3. With the smaller letters I used a mixture of yarns and wools in quite a random way, paying more attention to colours and where I wanted them. Again, wrap the tails of the wooltops around the letters and secure with a little glue at the back. Leave to dry.

TOP TIP

Letters are readily available online in different sizes and fonts. Spell out a word that means something to you.

Dig My Twig

When you're next out for a walk in the countryside, pick up a few twigs to make into cute little brooches. They are quick and easy and make great pressies. Alternatively, buy some tiny readymade grapevine wreaths, or try making your own interesting shapes from things in the garden. All you need to do is add some wooltops to bring them to life!

WHAT YOU'LL NEED

• Small amounts of wooltops and yarns in different colours

• A few small twigs – try to get some interesting shapes, and make sure they are not going to crumble too easily

• Tiny grapevine wreaths – I used heart-shaped and round ones

• Some strong glue suitable for use with wool

• Metal brooch backs

HOW TO MAKE

1. Pull off some small pieces of wooltops. If you are making a small brooch (no more than about 10cm/4in long and 1cm/½in wide), quite wispy pieces are good. You can always build up more on top but you don't want to make it too bulky and difficult to wind, plus it will stick much more easily if it's wispy.

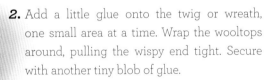

2. Add a little glue onto the twig or wreath, one small area at a time. Wrap the wooltops around, pulling the wispy end tight. Secure with another tiny blob of glue.

3. Keep adding the wool until the entire twig is covered, or leave little areas of twig showing here and there. Try different effects such as twisting two colours together to get a 'candy twist'. Or you can add a little yarn wrapped around over the top of the wooltops. Also try mixing a little Angelina glitter fibre into the wooltops for some extra sparkle!

4. When you're finished, add plenty of glue onto the back, near the top, and then carefully add the brooch back. Leave to dry completely.

Hang the Stash

Most of us are guilty of hoarding rather more wool and yarn than we actually really need, so here's a great idea for using up those leftovers.

WHAT YOU'LL NEED

• Curtain pole or a length of 15mm (½in) copper pipe about 15–20cm (6–8in) longer than the width of the door opening

• Yarns – I used a mixture of my own handspun yarns, Knit Collage Gypsy Garden, Noro Kureyon Air, Debbie Bliss Paloma, Mrs Moon Plump Superchunky, Sirdar Hayfield Chunky, Hedgehog Worsted in Genie and lots of other bits and bobs I had lying around, including a few pieces of pompom trim

• Sharp scissors

• 50–60 metal rings – I used split washers from the local farm shop

• Optional: flat-backed beads or cabochons and glue

• Curtain pole fixings or brackets

HOW TO MAKE

1. If you can, temporarily hang your pole above the door so you can slide the completed rings onto the pole to see the effect. If this isn't possible, suspend it somewhere else, or lay it out on the floor instead. If the pole is not hanging up in place, then measure the height of the doorway space so you know how long to cut the yarn.

2. Prepare the yarn for hanging by cutting off lengths that are either double or quadruple the height of your doorway. You can trim them a little later on if they are slightly too long. If the yarn is particularly fine, you may want quadruple lengths to add a bit more body to it.

3. If it's a double or quadruple length, fold into two or four accordingly and push the loop(s) through the metal ring by a few centimetres, then bring the ends though the loop and pull tight. If you only have a single length, just tie it on at the top. If a piece of yarn isn't quite long enough, just tie some bits together. Make a feature of the knots or bows!

4. Alternate colours and styles of yarn so not all one type of yarn is grouped into one place. Try tying some knots into groups of yarns too, to add further effect.

5. Add a little glue to your decorative beads or cabochons (if using) and curtain rings and wait for it to dry a little. Then press firmly together and leave to dry.

6. For the full effect, make finials, tassels and a tie-back (see pages 14–15), and then hang up your curtain pole with your chosen fixings or brackets.

ANYTHING GOES!

You can even introduce a few trimmings and ribbon into the mix too. If you don't have a curtain pole, use a cut-down broom handle to hang your stash!

Felted Finials, Tie-back & Tassels

WHAT YOU'LL NEED

For the finials

• Two 1m (1yd) lengths of wooltops and smaller bits of other colours to decorate – I used Pale Yellow Olive with Candy Pink

• Felting needle and a piece of foam

• Soapy water and soap

• Pencil

• Sharp craft knife or scalpel

• Fabric glue

For the tie-back

• 22mm (⅞ in) giant crochet hook

• 1m (1yd) wooltops – I used Glittery Unicorn blend

• Cup hook

• Optional: a few pompoms to decorate

FELT BALL FINIALS

1. Wet felt two large felt ball finials for each end of the pole in the colour of your choosing to match the curtain. See the Precious Pooch Pendant project on page 30 for instructions.

2. Leave the balls to dry, then needle felt some large polka dots on them here and there. See page 20 for needle felting instructions.

3. Press the end of the copper pipe or curtain pole firmly into the side of each ball so it indents slightly and makes a mark. If necessary trace around it with a pencil.

4. Take a sharp craft knife or scalpel and cut out a pole-sized hole in the side of each finial. Keep trimming the hole until the finial sits snugly onto the end of the pole. When it's up you can add a little glue to keep the finials in place!

TIE-BACK

1. Use the giant crochet hook to chain a length of wooltops to achieve a 'plaited' effect. Tie off each end when it's done. Attach a cup hook to the wall at one side, and squeeze two more metal rings (from making the curtain) onto the ends of the chained wooltops tie-back. Hook the tie-back around your curtain to hold it back when you need to.

2. Optional: dangle a few matching yarn pompoms from the tie-back too!

For the tassels

- Selection of wooltops and yarn odds and ends
  - Piece of strong card 10–15cm (4–6in) long
    - Tapestry, wool or weaving needle

TASSELS

1. Start by splitting up some wooltops and yarns vertically into narrow lengths of around 30cm (12in).

2. Wrap these lengths tightly around the cardboard. Keep wrapping different colours and lengths until you have enough for a tassel (see picture).

3. Thread the needle with a piece of strong yarn and pass the needle under the yarns at the very top edge. Tie a knot, leaving an end to hang the tassel by.

4. Remove the cardboard and then tie the yarn tightly around 2.5cm (1in) down from the top of the tassel, as pictured.

5. Trim the bottom of the tassel straight and it's ready to hang!

Whoop Whoop for the Hoop!

LEVEL
EASY ONCE YOU KNOW HOW

Use some simple embroidery stitches on backgrounds of fluffy wooltops to create sweet little wall art hoops.

WHAT YOU'LL NEED

To make one 15cm (6in) hoop

• Piece of hessian or open weave fabric to stitch onto, slightly larger than your hoop size

• Embroidery hoop – I used 15cm (6in) hoops

• Selection of wooltops, yarns and threads – odds and ends are great for this

• Tapestry, wool or weaving needle – the eye should be large enough to take your yarns but it also needs to be sharp enough to pierce the fabric

• Pins

• Sharp scissors

See page 18 for details of the stitches

HOW TO MAKE

Place the hessian or fabric in the hoop and secure by tightening the screw at the top. Keep it taut. When your picture is finished, trim the hessian tight at the back.

FOR THE LANDSCAPE PICTURE

Lay out wispy wooltops to mark out different areas of the picture. You can break it down into areas of 'sky' and 'grass', creating a horizon line too if that helps. Pin these pieces of wooltops in place while you stitch on top. French knots are great for making little flowers. Use contrasting colours to the green 'grassy' wooltops underneath. Also use bunched up pieces of wooltops in a flower colour and add a little French knot in the centre of each to hold in place. Use cross stitches and running stitches to add texture over the wool in the sky. Add some little stitches here and there to represent some beach huts too. Fill in areas between wooltops and yarns using an overstitch in different colours.

FOR THE FLOWERS PICTURE

Lay out the wooltops for the vase in the bottom half of the frame. Shape it into a round base. Don't use too much. You can always layer up more if you need it, so keep it wispy. Use a couple of different coloured blues here to add shadow to the base. Attach to the hessian using a mixture of cross stitches and running stitches using matching (or contrasting) threads. To make the flowers, coil up small amounts of wooltops in reds, pinks, yellows and purples. Do one at a time, and each time sew down with a French knot in the centre. Add running stitches around the circle of each flower. Add stems and leaves using green wooltops or yarns, and again sew them down with running stitch or cross stitch.

Whoop Whoop for the Hoop!

FOR THE CACTUS PICTURE

Lay out the wooltops for the pot first in the bottom third of the space. Use a mixture of orange and yellow, shading it on one side. Tuck the wooltops in so you have a neat shape. Fix it down with a backstitch in orange thread to indicate horizontal stripes. Now add blue French knot 'polka dots' on top and outline the darker edge with a blue backstitch. Shape out some green wooltops for the cactus. There are three main shapes here – use a mixture of different greens for greater effect. Attach the wooltops down to the hessian with lots of small running stitches to indicate the prickles – I used a contrasting green yarn for this. Add a backstitch outline in a darker green on one side. Finish by adding three little cactus flowers in bright pink at the top of each segment. If you can shape them into little hearts then do so, otherwise, blobs will fine. Add a red French knot in the centre of each and another yellow French knot on the top of each, pushing down the middle of the heart shape.

TOP TIP

You can also work straight onto shop-bought or handmade felt if you want to keep things woolly. Likewise try using other cottons and fabrics once you no longer need the open holes to guide your needle!

THE STITCHES

Running stitch The easiest of stitches, where the needle goes into the fabric and comes out again at an equal distance. Looks the same on the front and the back.

Backstitch This is just like a 'joined up' running stitch. Each time your needle comes up for air, stitch back to the end of the last stitch. This is great for continuous lines.

Cross stitch Use the holes in the fabric to create little crosses. Simply stitch a diagonal from left to right, and then cross the next stitch back over the top in the opposite direction. Line up the stitch with the holes in the fabric to make them uniform and square, or ignore the holes if you are feeling defiant and alternative!

Overstitch This is sort of half of the cross stitch – just going in one of the directions and repeated over and over with the stitches all next to one another and slanting.

French knot Thread the yarn through the fabric from the back to the front. Hold the yarn taut just above the hessian. The tension is important! With the needle just in front of the yarn, wind the yarn around the needle a couple of times. Re-insert the needle tip just next to where it last emerged and then carefully pull the French knot tight.

Soaping, Rubbing and Stabbing Fluff into Stuff (aka Felting)

Needle Felting

Needle felting is a dry felting technique that uses very sharp, barbed needles to push fibres up and down until they start to tangle and bond together. It is great for decorating felt with fine details, joining felt together, and ideal for sculpting and making solid shapes, so works well in combination with wet felting. Although the process is very different from wet felting, the end result is the same – felted wool that has matted together and shrunk.

DECORATING AND EMBELLISHING

Decorations and details can be added onto felt using small amounts of wispy wool. Keep the felting needle perpendicular and stab gently to avoid needle breakage, making sure the barbs on the needle travel through. As the wool disappears into the felt, build up designs gradually. If you don't like what you've done, it's easy to pick off the wool with the end of the needle and start again! Use this method for the fluffy felt pieces on page 34.

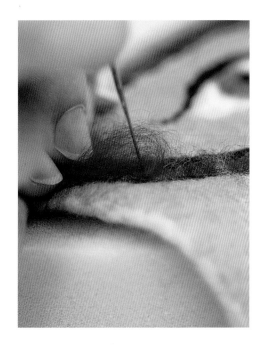

BEFORE YOU START

When needle felting onto a flat piece of felt or fabric, place foam underneath it to protect the work surface.

WHAT YOU'LL NEED

• Wooltops

• Felting needles

• Foam

FELTING NEEDLES

Felting needles come in several different sizes. I use two sizes – a 38 gauge star profile needle for faster general work and decoration, and a larger 36 gauge triangular needle for coarser 3D work.

SCULPTING AND SHAPING

When making 3D shapes, needle felted wool will shrink as the fibres become entangled and air is removed. Tightly bunch together wooltops in the rough shape you need, and start to stab together. (It is often easier and quicker at this stage to use a multi-needle tool with four large needles if it's a large piece.) Add on more wool as required and refine the shape as much as possible. This takes time and patience! When the overall shape has been achieved, you can refine it using just one needle. Repeated stabbing with one needle will create indentations, which is useful for detailing (use this method for the pincushion on page 26).

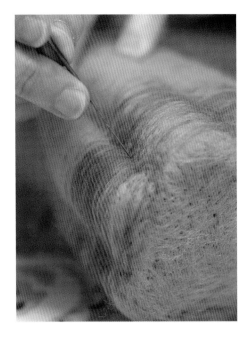

RAISED NEEDLE FELTING

By using slightly more wool and needling slightly less, you will find it is possible to create decorative raised areas – as on some of the pendants (page 24) and the pincushion (page 26). Bunch up smaller pieces of wooltops and needle to form 'raised bumps' by needling more around the edges of each bump rather than all over it.

WARNING

Felting needles are extremely sharp and not suitable for children to use. Take care not to stab yourself!

Wet Felting: Simple Flat Felt

Flat felt is the easiest sort to make and a good place to start if you've never felted before. Wooltops are separated and laid out into layers and patterns before being covered with netting and rubbed with soap and water. After the fibres have started to bond together, a series of rinsing and rolling in a bamboo mat further shrinks and hardens the felt.

BEFORE YOU START

• • • • • • • • • • •

• Decide on the size of the finished piece, remembering it will shrink by 15–20%.

• Get your wool and equipment ready, and protect your work surface, as it will get wet.

• Work on a bamboo mat, or directly onto a waterproof worktop.

WET FELTING KIT

• • • • • • • • • • •

• Wooltops (50g/1¾oz will make a 20cm/8in square piece of flat felt)

• Netting

• Squirty bottle

• Washing up liquid/bar of soap

• Dishcloth and towel

• Bamboo mat

• Hot/cold running water

HOW TO DO IT

• •

1. Hold the wooltops about 15cm (6in) from the end in one hand. Release the very ends of the fibres with your other hand. The wool should come away easily and be fine, even and wispy.

2. Lay the wool down with all the fibres facing the same direction, overlapping slightly, building up a fine, even layer. Use enough wool so you can no longer see through it to the surface beneath.

3. Add a second layer of wooltops, facing in the opposite direction. This will make it thicker, and also make it shrink more evenly.

4. Lay the netting over the fibres and use a squirty bottle to sprinkle soapy water over the netting. Hold the netting taut with one hand. Use your other hand to spread the soapy water through with a dishcloth. It is important that all air is

removed and the fibres are flat and wet. It should feel as if the wool is stuck to the table with soapy glue: if it feels springy, more soapy water is needed; if it feels puddly and over-wet, mop up a little! Rub a bar of soap over the netting to make it slippery. The soap encourages the felting by getting the microscopic scales on the wool fibres to swell, move open and eventually lock together.

5. Keeping the netting flat and taut, rub with both hands and plenty of pressure for about ten minutes. Some fibres may cling to the net as you rub. If they do, peel back the net, remove the fibres and replace the net in a slightly different position to prevent permanent adherence.

6. Test if the felt is sufficiently rubbed: remove netting and briskly rub your hand across it. If the fibres no longer move, you are done. If any areas wobble or seem delicate, replace the net and continue to rub until everything is well held together. This is important!

7. Rinse under running lukewarm water. Do not immerse or leave under the tap for too long as the felt is still very delicate. Wring gently. Repeat several times until most of the soap is removed. Squeeze out excess water.

8. To further shrink and harden the felt, it is rolled in a bamboo mat. This provides friction as it pushes back and forth against the slats. Roll up the felt tightly and place a towel under the mat to stop it sliding about.

9. The felt will shrink more in the direction it is rolled in, so to achieve even shrinkage, keep rotating the felt as you roll. Roll the mat back and forth with a firm, even pressure about twenty times. Unroll, turn the felt 90° clockwise and then repeat. Continue through 360°, then turn over and repeat all rolling on the other side.

10. Rinse again using hotter water and then very cold. Once soap-free, squeeze out as much water as possible and repeat the rolling process. Lay flat to dry naturally; finish with a warm iron if desired.

The Resplendent Pendant

Make these little needle felted necklaces using small amounts of felt and wooltops. They make unique gifts!

WHAT YOU'LL NEED

• Cabochon pendant shapes to set your felted pieces into

• Small pieces of shop-bought or handmade felt to work onto

• Sharp scissors

• Small amounts of wooltops in different colours – see 'How to make' for specific project requirements

• 38g felting needle and foam

• Fabric glue

• Chain lengths with closures or waxed cord

See page 20 for needle felting instructions

HOW TO MAKE

1. Cut a piece of felt slightly bigger than the setting. It may shrink a little as you are needle felting, and you can always trim it later!

2. Referring to page 20, needle tiny amounts of wooltops and build designs up gradually. It's nice to build up a 'mound' of wool and make the pendants slightly 3D with gently protruding elements – they needn't be completely flat.

3. Once each piece is finished, trim it so it's still SLIGHTLY larger than the setting.

4. Glue your piece into the setting. Use lots of glue and poke the edges inside the setting. If there is still any felt hanging out, snip it off with scissors.

5. Leave to dry, then string onto a matching chain or wax cord.

FOR THE TOADSTOOL Working onto green felt, needle the toadstool top in Bright Red with Cherry Red low lights, and then add tiny White spots. Finally add the toadstool stem in White.

FOR THE DAFFODIL Working onto turquoise felt, add a little Bright Yellow circle for the centre of the daffodil, and then five further circles at equal distances around the outside for the petals. Add an Orange centre and a Christmas Green stem.

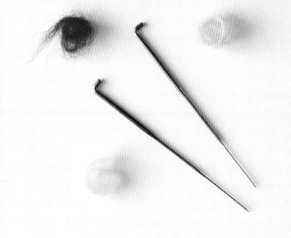

FOR THE CUPCAKE Working onto pink felt, needle a cupcake base using Pale Blue, and carefully outline it with Regal Purple, adding a few vertical lines to indicate the paper case. Next add a White cake, with a Cherry Red cherry on top. Add yellow Angelina sparkles at the base of the cake.

FOR THE SHEEP Working onto white felt, add the shape of the sheep's head using Black. Add ears either side of the oval head, then two tiny White eyes with Black centres.

FOR THE FLOWER GARDEN Working onto green felt, add small amounts of Bright Red, Bright Yellow and Candy Pink circles for the little flowers. Add even smaller flower centres using Bright Yellow and Black. Add some longer shapes in Lilac, Regal Purple and Flamingo Pink to indicate longer spikes of flowers. Add Grass Green leaves and stems here and there until you are happy. I also used small amounts of White, Orange, Delphinium and Hot Pink.

FOR THE LADYBIRD Working onto red felt, add the Black section at one end for the head. Add White spots. Then add Black spots on the wings and finally the fine vertical Black line down the centre.

Keep Off the Lawn Pincushion

Grace any craft room with this useful pincushion made from wooltops and sculpted into a charming vintage cup and saucer. Make a tiny toadstool to sit on your pincushion or a larger one that is big enough for the fairies to hide underneath!

WHAT YOU'LL NEED

For a 6 x 5cm (2¼ x 2in) toadstool

• 6–10g (¼– ½oz) or 15cm (6in) White wooltops plus a few bits for the spots

• Foam

• 36g felting needle

• 38g felting needle

• 6–10g (¼– ½oz) or 15cm (6in) Cherry Red wooltops plus a few bits for joining

See page 20 for needle felting instructions

LEVEL

EASY ONCE YOU KNOW HOW

HOW TO MAKE THE TOADSTOOLS

1. To make the base of the large toadstool, tightly coil some white wooltops into a shape measuring around 5 x 2cm (2 x ¾in) and start to needle together using the larger 36g needle.

2. As the base starts to come together, change over to the finer 38g needle. Keep turning it and refining it until it measures around 4cm (1½in) long and just under 2cm (¾in) wide. If you can, needle it so it is slightly wider at one end. Keep going until it feels firm and well felted.

3. For the top, fold some red wooltops into a roughly circular 'pad' measuring just over 5cm (2in). Start to needle using the 36g needle, and move over to the 38g needle again once it starts to come together. Keep needling until it has reduced in size and becomes firmer, rotating and turning as you go.

4. Start to shape the top so that it becomes slightly cup-shaped and work more into the underside of the cup, making a lip at the edge. Keep needling until it feels firm and well felted.

5. Coil up small wisps of white wooltops into little circles and needle them onto the top here and there.

6. Turn the mushroom top over and put the base in place. Add a little fresh red wooltops around the top of the base and needle the two pieces together until they are well attached.

7. Turn the toadstool the right way up again and needle the top some more to get ride of any fibres that may have poked through during the joining process. As well as the large one, make a slightly smaller version of this toadstool to put on top of your pincushion like I did.

WHAT YOU'LL NEED

For the pincushion

• Approx. 25g (1oz) or 1m (1yd) of Lettuce Green wooltops or enough for your needle felted ball to fit into the cup snugly – this may vary according to the size of your cup!

• Cup and saucer

• Foam

• 36g felting needle

• 38g felting needle

• Multi-needle felting tool (optional, but will speed things up!)

• 6–10g (¼– ½oz) or 15cm (6in) Racing Green wooltops for the scallop fence

• Small needle felted toadstool (see page 26)

• Small amounts of Yellow, Orange, Cherry Red, Gold, Turquoise, Lilac, Candy Pink and White wooltops

• Glue

TOP TIP

Remember, the more you needle into the felt, the more it will 'indent' – so if you have areas that look too uneven and lumpy, simply needle them more to even them out.

HOW TO MAKE THE PINCUSHION

1. Coil up the green wooltops into a ball shape as tightly as you can. It should seem slightly too big to fit into your cup, as once it's well needle felted it will get quite a bit smaller. Make sure it is coiled up with a smooth even 'coat' on the outside, so there aren't any 'cracks' or joins in the wool.

2. Working on some foam, hold the ball as tightly as you can in one hand and start to needle the ball together with the larger 36g needle. Keep turning it and rotating it to keep it an even round shape otherwise it will quickly turn into a squashed egg!

3. Switch over to the finer 38g needle, and if you have a multi-needle tool, experiment with this as it will speed up the needle felting of the ball. Either way, keep needling until the ball is REALLY well felted and firm.

4. Now start to 'sculpt' the top of the ball by adding in some lines, starting at the front and flaring out to the back of one side of the ball. Decide which part of the ball looks best, as this should be uppermost.

5. Using the 38g needle, loosely needle some yellow wooltops in very fine lines, as pictured, until you get the spacing right. When you are happy with the spacing switch over to the larger 36g needle and really needle down into the ball. If the yellow wool starts to completely disappear, simply add more over the top until you achieve the desired effect. The more you needle down into the ball, the more distinct the sculptural effect.

6. Keeping the ball upright, start to plan out where the scalloped fence will sit. Attach the darker green wooltops with the 38g needle loosely to start with until you've gone all the way around. It's easiest to take small wisps of dark green wool and coil them around into circles, which are then 'butted' together.

7. Once the shape is looking about right, add more wool on top to make the colour more solid and opaque. Now move over to the larger 36g needle again and really sculpt down into the ball, creating a ridge at the edge of each scallop. Again, the more you needle in with this larger needle, the more pronounced the edge will become.

8. Next add the little toadstool in place by using some new white or green wooltops around its base. Needle until secure.

9. Take tiny pieces of different colours and coil them up into tiny round flowers. Add them here and there randomly as shown in the picture. Again, if you want them to be more sculptural, needle around the edge of each one with the larger 36g needle once they are attached.

10. Make the larger yellow flower separately by needling together a small circle of yellow wooltops on top of a piece of foam. Once it's well felted, cut it into shape using sharp scissors. Attach it to the pincushion by needling a small orange centre into the middle of the flower once it's in place.

11. Glue the pincushion in place in the cup.

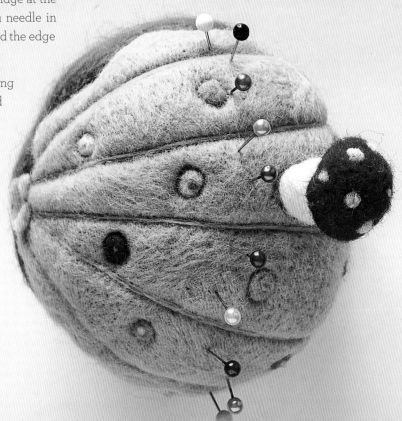

Precious Pooch Pendant

Your canine chum will look remarkably fetching modelling this special doggie felt ball necklace. Turn it into more of a collar with a stronger strand running through the middle. And why not make a matching one for yourself?!

WHAT YOU'LL NEED

· ·

For a necklace measuring approx. 14cm (5½in)

- Tape measure

- Around twelve pieces of wooltops approx. 5g (¼oz) or 15–20cm (6–8in) long for each ball – increase or decrease according to the size of your dog's neck. I made each ball a different colour and used a mixture of: Bright Yellow, Flamingo, Cherry Red, Hot Pink, Rose Pink, Candy Pink, Gold, Fairy Floss Fantasia (blend), Salmon Pink, Peach and hand-dyed (see page 76)

- Warm water and a squirt of washing up liquid in a squirty bottle

- Bar of soap

- Small bamboo mat (optional)

- Thick beading elastic – about 50cm (20in)

- Tapestry, wool or weaving needle

- Small pliers

- Glue

- Multi-needle felting tool and some foam

- Sharp scissors

See page 20 for needle felting instructions

Precious Pooch Pendant

HOW TO MAKE

1. Measure your dog's neck to get a rough idea of how many felt balls you'll need to make. Each ball should end up about 2.5–3cm (1–1¼in) in diameter, so calculate how many you'll need and make sure you have the right number of wooltops pieces, all the same length.

2. Prepare the soapy water and have the soap to hand. Start to coil up the first pieces of wooltops in your hands as tightly as possible, making sure you finish with a smooth continuous piece of wool around the outside so there are no joins or crevices. Splay out the very ends of the fibres and use them like a little jacket around the very outside of the ball.

3. Hold the ball tightly in one hand, and sprinkle the soapy water over the top until the ball is saturated all the way through to the core. Wring out excess water.

4. Very carefully, cover the ball with more soap from the bar of soap and very, very GENTLY start to roll the ball in your palms. If you press too hard at this point, or don't have enough soap, you run the risk of channels appearing in the ball. The tighter you coil it up in the first place, and the soapier you get it and the more gently you roll it, the easier it will be! If it does develop some unwanted channels and start to resemble a small brain, add more soap and persevere.

5. Continue to roll gently in your palms until the ball starts to harden slightly (this should take about five minutes), and then start to roll it on a harder work surface, or ideally a bamboo mat if you have one. Keep the soap levels up, right through the rolling process, as this will make the bead 'felt' and become hard more quickly.

6. Once the bead is rock hard and well felted, rinse it well under the tap in lukewarm water, taking care to remove ALL the soap. Leave to dry completely.

7. Repeat the same process with the other pieces of wooltops, so you end up with felt beads that are roughly the same size.

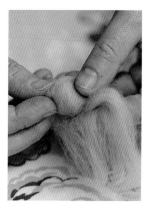

8. Take the length of stretchy elastic and thread it through the sharp needle. Thread the beads onto the elastic by pushing the needle through them – it is helpful to have a pair of pliers to pull the needle through with. It is also easier to do this when the beads are completely dry.

9. Check the necklace for size around your furry friend's neck, then tie the elastic in a secure knot, and add a blob of glue. Leave to dry.

10. To make the bone shaped 'tag', layer up some wooltops onto the foam into a small rectangle shape. Use a multi-needle felting tool to needle the wooltops together. Keep turning it over and carry on needling until it is well felted and no longer fluffy. This can take about ten minutes.

11. Make a paper template first if you need one, or just cut a bone shape out of the felt. To do this, start by cutting a fat sausage shape. Next taper the middle of each side, and finally round off the bone parts at the top and bottom.

12. If you like, needle felt your dog's name (or shorter nickname!) onto the tag using wooltops in a contrasting colour. Attach the tag by sewing it on a loop around the cord, and you're done!

TOP TIP

The felt balls are very resilient to dirt but if the felt ball necklace does get caked in mud, wash it with a bit of soap and rinse under a lukewarm tap – it won't hurt!

Fluffy Felt

Who remembers Fuzzy Felt? I think I spent many an hour creating pictures with little pieces of felt as a child. Maybe that's where my subconscious fluffy love affair started – all those years ago!

WHAT YOU'LL NEED

• Handmade or shop-bought sheets of felt, in various colours, enough to cut out the templates on pages 78–79

LEVEL
EASY ONCE YOU KNOW HOW

• Wooltops – I used small amounts in Bright Red, Bright Yellow, White, Turquoise, British Racing Green, Orange and Black

• 36g felting needle and some foam

• Sharp scissors

See page 20 for needle felting instructions

See page 22 for wet felting instructions (to make handmade felt)

HOW TO MAKE

1. Trace around the templates and cut out the felt shapes you need – I varied the shape and height of my pots. You'll also need a background piece 45 x 32.5cm (17¾ x 12¾in); and a rectangle and strips for the window: 13.5 x 10cm (5⅓ x 4in); 17 x 1.5cm (6¾ x ⅔in); 13.5 x 1cm (5⅓ x ⅓in) and 10 x 1cm (4 x ⅓in).

2. Add the needle felt details. Starting with the four cacti, following the picture from left to right, needle felt dark green vertical lines on the first cactus. Keep the wooltops fine and wispy and only stab the needle in where you want to see the lines. Add some tiny little yellow spots on top of the green lines here and there. Needle fine white lines onto the second cactus, following the lines of the 'arms'. Needle small white spots onto the third cactus and small yellow spots onto the fourth cactus.

3. For the pots, following the picture from left to right, needle orange spots onto the blue pot, a yellow scalloped edge onto the red pot, some turquoise spots onto the gold pot and some horizontal red stripes onto the pink pot.

4. Needle felt some centres into the flowers using small coils of wooltops in yellow, black or white, and some vertical green lines onto the tulip. Piece together everything as per the picture and let your child get creative.

TOP TIP

Not suitable for very small children under 3 years of age as they may choke on the felt pieces.

Watercolour Corsages

Make pretty little clusters of flowers from plain, blended and hand-dyed wooltops. If you don't want to make your own felt, you can use readymade instead!

WHAT YOU'LL NEED

• Handmade or shop-bought sheets of felt, green for the leaves, and whatever you choose for the flowers – I used hand-dyed Malabrigo Nube wooltops in colour Arco Iris

LEVEL
PRETTY DAMN EASY

• Sharp scissors

• Fabric glue

• Stamens (optional)

• Needle and thread (optional)

• Buttons or beads (optional)

• Felting needle, foam and small bits of wooltops (optional)

See page 20 for needle felting instructions

See page 22 for wet felting instructions (to make handmade felt)

TOP TIP

I felted the flower colours and the leaf colours at the same time into one big piece of flat felt.

HOW TO MAKE

1. Make as many pieces of flat wet felt as required. A piece of felt around 20 x 20cm (8 x 8in) will make all the flowers pictured, and you'll need a slightly smaller piece for the leaves.

2. To make the flowers, simply cut out different sized circles from the felt. Either make a little paper template to do this, or just do it by eye. I used circles that were approx. 3cm (1¼in) and 5cm (2in).

3. To make the petals, make four small snips around the edge of the felt circle with small sharp scissors at 12 o'clock, 3 o'clock, 6 o'clock and 9 o'clock. Don't make these cuts too deep, else they'll meet in the middle and the whole thing will fall apart!

4. To make a four petalled flower, simply 'round off' the petals at the sides of each snip. To make an eight petalled flower, just add an extra snip in between the four before rounding off, and so on! It's as simple as that!

5. If you have some stamens, sew them around the centre. I also added diamante beads into the very middle. An alternative is to needle felt a little centre into the flower. Simply take some contrasting wooltops, and needle into place gently. Be sure to work on some protective foam when you're doing this.

6. Cut leaf shapes from the green felt, and either glue or sew into place underneath.

7. Add clusters of these flowers together to make a larger corsage, or use single flowers for decoration on other projects. Adding a little brooch bar on the back means you can attach the corsage to anything you like – perhaps a scarf, hat, lapel or bag.

Jaw Dropper Shopper

Take this bag to market and stand out from the crowd! Layers of wool are laid around the template. Once the wool starts to felt and shrink, the top is cut open and the template removed to leave a seamless 3D shape.

WHAT YOU'LL NEED

For a bag that measures 26cm (10in) high and 39cm (15½in) at widest point

• Wooltops: layer one (inside) approx. 75g (3oz) Aubergine; layer two (middle) approx. 50g (2oz) Black; layer three (outer) 75g (3oz) Black; small amounts of wooltops and curly wool locks in different colours for the flower design

• Wet felting kit (see page 22)

• Sharp scissors

• Handles – I used black polka dot leather-look

LEVEL
LESS EASY BUT YOU CAN DO IT!

See page 22 for wet felting instructions

Enlarge the template on page 78 and cut out of plastic.

HOW TO MAKE

1. Lay the template on the table and, using half of the Aubergine wooltops, pull off the ends of the fibres with your fingertips and lay wispy fibres vertically over the template until it is covered. Add an overlap of a couple of centimetres all around the edge.

2. Cover with netting and sprinkle soapy solution over the top to wet through. Remove excess water and rub a bar of soap across the top. It should feel sudsy and soapy. Rub with both hands using a firm pressure for a few minutes. Remove the net, turn over and fold in the edges as tightly and neatly as possible.

3. Repeat steps 1–2 using the rest of the Aubergine wool on the other side. Remove the net and turn over. Fold in the edges.

4. Repeat step 1 using half of the 50g Black wooltops, but lay the fibres more finely and horizontally. Repeat on the other side as before. Remove the netting, turn over and fold in the edges.

5. Split the final 75g piece of Black wooltops in half. Using the first half, lay some fibres vertically, then horizontally (this is to even out the shrinkage). Make a larger overlap this time.

6. Now for the design! You can go freestyle here if you want to. The KEY is to use TINY bits of wool. Don't twiddle it together too much. Leave it quite 'open' or it won't rub together later. Shape the wool into circles for petals, or ovals with pinched ends for leaves. Lay them onto the black background as follows.

   • Add stalks first – it's easier to sit the flowers on top.

   • Add Pale Pink petals for the tiger lily. Add tiny bits of Rose Pink wool down each petal for veins, tiny spots in Cherry Red and stamens in Citrus Green. Add a few small leaves.

• Add a poppy using Bright Red, Cherry Red and some curly wool locks, with Black wool in the centre.

• For the yellow flower use the palest yellow colours to lay out the petals. Add darker shades and brown over the top for shading. Add an orange centre.

• For the purple flowers, use a mix of Delphinium, Cornflower and Lilac in tiny blobs either side of a Bright Olive stem.

• Add more flowers and leaves here and there. Finish with small Turquoise spots in between the shrubbery!

7. Repeat step 2 but this time rub for at least 30 minutes or until the fibres are well fixed together. If they are still moving around, rub for longer and make sure it's soapy!

8. Turn over and fold in the larger edges. Repeat the last Black layer on the other side, but this time with NO overlap. Add more Black wooltops around the sides to hide any 'edges'. Don't let it hang over the bag edge.

9. Repeat step 2 until all the fibres are REALLY WELL fixed. Rub the bag without the netting, using plenty of soap. Rub around the edges until it feels robust, slightly smaller, well-felted and 'rougher' to the touch.

10. Follow steps 7–9 on page 23 to rinse and roll the bag. Then rinse again in hotter water and repeat the rolling ten times horizontally and ten times vertically on both sides. Cut into the top corner to find the template, then cut right across the top of the bag, open it up and remove the template. Trim and neaten up the edges if necessary.

11. Rub the newly cut edges with soapy water and soap for about five minutes until well-felted. Form a 'base' at the bottom of the bag for it to sit on, and rub and shape this using plenty of soap.

12. Rinse in warm water, then freezing cold, taking care to remove ALL the soap. It should have shrunk quite a lot now. If it hasn't, rinse again using hotter water.

13. Wring, roll again in the mat and leave to dry.

14. Sew handles to the inside of the felt bag, so as not to obstruct your lovely design, and leave to dry.

Weaving Fluff In and Out of Stuff

You can buy a simple loom quite cheaply or try making one if you fancy having a go before parting with any cash – the best way is a picture frame with parallel nails across the top and bottom. You could even use cardboard with slits cut top and bottom.

WHAT YOU'LL NEED

• Simple table-top loom

• Warping thread or yarn – I used 12/9 medium cotton tapestry weaving thread

• Different coloured wooltops and yarns to weave with

• Fork or comb

• Sharp scissors

• Dowel or driftwood or hanger to display your weaving and loop it onto

• Tapestry, wool or weaving needle – not essential but makes life easier sometimes with finer yarns

KEY WORDS

The WARP refers to the vertical threads through which you weave the horizontal WEFT threads that make up your weaving. It's easy to get these mixed up – a good way to remember is the word warp looks like the word 'harp' and a harp always has vertical strings! And 'weft' rhymes with 'left' and your warp threads go horizontally from left to right or right to left.

HOW TO WARP THE LOOM

Adding the vertical warp threads to weave between.

1. Use a really strong warp thread or string. It shouldn't have any 'give' in it so it can be used very tightly without stretching. Cotton thread is best here. Work out how much you need by measuring the length of the loom and multiplying it by the number of verticals. You don't need to use the full width of the loom – you can just warp up a central portion.

2. Tie the thread off tightly around the top left hook or corner of the loom and then start to hook it around each end up and down, keeping it as TIGHT as you possibly can. Keeping it tight and taut is really important and will give you better results.

3. Tie it off TIGHTLY on the last hook and cut.

HOW TO WEAVE THE WEFT

Adding the main body of the weave horizontally over and under the warp threads.

1. A knotted 'fringe' at the base of the weaving helps secure the end when you remove it from the loom. To make a wooltops fringe, gather equal lengths of wooltops of about one pencil width. Straddle the first two warp threads, then feed the ends from either side back through the middle. Pull down tight and continue across the row. (If you have a single warp thread remaining, just leave it – you won't notice it at the end!)

2. Now you're ready to start weaving. Weaving is very easy if you remember a few key points:

- Weave 'under' a vertical warp thread and then 'over' the next vertical warp thread all the way across the row. On the next row, it is the opposite: over then under. Each row should always be the opposite of the one before.

- Don't pull the wool too tightly. Go across the row in an 'arc', then push the yarns down with a fork or a comb. Keep the wool relatively loose or it will pull in at the sides and will look misshapen when you've finished.

- Ends of yarns can be tied on at the side when you start or finish a colour, but it's neater to leave them hanging and then weave them in at the back using a wool needle.

TOP TIP

Wooltops and chunky yarns make your weaving grow much faster than fine yarns! Yarns will give you a tighter weave, but with wooltops and other fibres you can add more interesting textures to your weaving.

Weaving Fluff In and Out of Stuff

3. To add tassels using yarn – cut yarn into about six 15cm (6in) lengths (you can change this later once you've mastered it). Straddle the first two warp threads with the centre of your bundle, then feed the ends from both sides back through the middle. Pull down and tie tightly. Repeat along the row.

4. Wait until you've woven a few more rows, then you can cut the little fringe to reveal more of what was underneath.

5. Experiment with different effects by 'bunching up' the wooltops in between the warp threads. This gives more texture and will add interest.

6. Remember that you don't need to weave right to the top of the warp threads and can finish it at any time when you think it looks balanced. When you've finished your weaving, carefully unhook the bottom first. The wooltops knots at the base may need tightening and should hold without tying. If you haven't used knots, you will need to cut and tie the bottom of each loop. At the top, carefully unhook each pair of threads and snip at the top. Tie tightly and either trim and tie over a piece of dowel or a little hanger for the wall. If you have woven right to the top of the warp threads, you can slip off each pair straight onto a hanger.

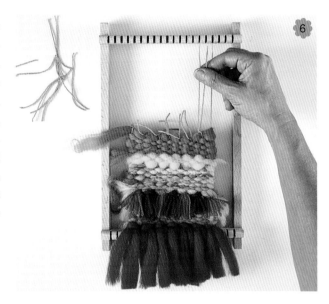

WOOLTOPS TASSEL HEART

For the wooltops wall hanging project, I Fluffy Heart You, on page 50.

1. Make one single piece of wooltops 'tassel' in the middle two warp threads.

2. Then carry on as per the diagram, left: two knots above, then three above, then four above, and finally one knot in the middle of each of the pairs of four.

Fluffy Flower Power

Get the kids to try this easy version of weaving on a paper plate and see it grow fast using wooltops, plus some regular yarn too if you fancy!

WHAT YOU'LL NEED

For one flower power plate

- Plastic or paper plate in any colour or design
- Pencil and ruler
- Sharp scissors
- Selection of wooltops – about 50cm (approx. 20in) of plenty of different colours
- String or strong yarn in any colour, or a mixture

HOW TO MAKE

1. On the back of the plate, mark an UNEVEN number of equal-sized sections around the edge by drawing straight lines across the plate, going through the centre each time. I split mine into seventeen sections.

2. Make each of the sections into a petal by cutting scallop shapes with some small scissors.

3. Take some strong yarn or string and string across between two opposite petals. Tie off at the back of the plate, leaving a tail. Then continue to string across opposite petals all the way around the flower – keeping it taut!

4. When all the 'petals' are strung, make a small hole in the centre of the plate. Push the remaining string through this hole to the back and tie it off securely to the tail from step 3. Now you're ready to weave!

5. Split your wooltops into four to six pieces, each about 20–30cm (8–12in) long. It's up to you how you use the wooltops – the chunkier each piece of wool, the quicker your weaving will grow!

6. Secure the first piece against the string in the very centre and then simply use your fingers to push it under and over each piece of string, working around the plate.

7. To change colour, just tie the two ends of the wooltops together gently and push the little knot through and underneath to the back of the weaving where you won't see it. Or, just leave a little tail poking behind of the new colour and carry on without pulling it too hard. When your weaving is finished, you can hide these tails more easily if they are still sticking out.

8. To finish, tie the last piece to the string and push through to the back to give a neat edge.

9. If you don't want to leave the plate on your finished piece, you can snip the wool or string at the edges and tie each front and back piece into a knot to make a little mat or hanging instead.

TOP TIP

Try experimenting by adding some yarns or ribbons into the weave! You could also try painting or decorating the plate first.

Shady Lady

This woven lampshade couldn't be simpler. Use different colours of wooltops or yarns to complement your décor and simply weave them in and out of the warp.

WHAT YOU'LL NEED

• New or recycled lampshade frame – I used a 20 x 20cm (8 x 8in) shade

• Strong cotton yarn for stringing up the warp – I used approx. 5m (5½yd) of cream warp cotton

• Selection of wooltops and yarns in different colours – I used approx. 130g (4½oz) wooltops in: Pinky Minky, Flamingo, Candy, White, Lettuce Green and Glittery Unicorn blend

• Trimmings (optional)

• Yarn

• Tapestry, wool or weaving needle

LEVEL
CHILD's PLAY

ADDING IN YARNS

You don't need to just use wooltops in your weave. Add in some other yarns or trimmings to mix it up a bit. The more, the merrier!

HOW TO MAKE

1. Start by warping up your shade. Tie the cotton to the top of the frame and then wind it around the frame, going from top to bottom, leaving about a 4cm (1½in) gap between each vertical thread. Tie off the first thread when you get back to the beginning. It's good to have an uneven number of threads as this will make it slightly easier to weave.

2. Take your first piece of wooltops and split it into about three or four pieces lengthways. The thicker the wooltops, the quicker your woven lampshade will grow.

3. Weave the end of it under the first warp thread and over the next, then keep going around until you reach the end of the piece. If you want to create a solid block of colour, then use another piece the same colour straight away. If you want variation or stripes, then change colour.

4. As you weave in and out, keep pushing the wooltops down to the bottom of the frame and make it as tight as possible. This way, it will hide most of your warp threads.

5. Keep weaving the wooltops in and out until you reach the top of the shade. Tidy up any loose ends by weaving them through to the inside of the frame.

6. Decide which way up you will use the shade, then choose a matching or contrasting yarn to sew around the top of the frame to hide the frame. Use a weaving needle to do this.

7. Either repeat at the base in the same way, or sew on some trimmings instead – I used a woven trim and a mini pompom trim attached with yarn.

Too Cool for Stool

Fancy putting your feet up on this cheeky little woven footstool after the day is done? It's great for small people to sit on too!

WHAT YOU'LL NEED

For a 34 x 29cm (13½ x 11½in) stool

- Wooden footstool frame

- Selection of wooltops in different colours – I used approx. 3m (3¼yd) Fairy Floss Fantasia blend, 1.5m (1¾yd) each of Peppermint Green, Peach, Pale Yellow Olive and Pale Turquoise

- Sewing needle and sharp scissors

- Strong cotton warp thread

- Felt flowers and leaves (see page 36)

- A few tiny pompoms to decorate the base (optional)

TOP TIP

The amount of wooltops you will need to use depends on the size of the stool – increase or decrease accordingly! I also used a few lengths of different random yarns, caught in with the wooltops.

LEVEL
PRETTY DAMN EASY

HOW TO MAKE

1. Start by warping up the stool frame using the warp thread. The reason for this is purely functional – it will make the weave on top much stronger and therefore allow you to sit on it! Without this warp, the wooltops may sag a little.

2. Tie the warp thread tightly onto the top of the frame at the longer end. Wrap the warp thread around each end as tightly as you can around six to eight times and tie off securely. It doesn't really matter what this looks like as no one will see it, but keep it TIGHT!

3. Follow this with the wooltops 'warp' next to and around it, using the Fairy Floss Fantasia blend. Secure at one end, and add around seven lengths back and forth. Secure tightly at the other end and keep as taut as possible without causing it to break.

4. Add the weft colours. Each time you add a colour, secure it underneath by tying. This can be fiddly, but you won't see it! Weave it over, under, over, under and so on, until you have used it up. Keep it as tight as possible. Take it to the back and tie to the next colour, taking care to keep the knots below!

5. Repeat using the other colours until you reach the end. I did about twenty-two rows of weaving.

6. Secure carefully underneath and weave or tie in any ends so none is visible from above.

7. Add your decorations: make sure they are secure if they'll be sat on! Sew or glue the felt flowers and leaves to the top or make some tiny yarn pompoms to tie onto the wooden struts at the base of the stool.

I Fluffy Heart You

Wooltops weaving is very relaxing, a whole lot easier than you might imagine and much more forgiving than weaving with yarns. Remember the mantra: 'under, over, under, over'.

WHAT YOU'LL NEED

• Loom of any size – I used one approx. 20 x 10cm (8 x 4in)

• Selection of wooltops in different colours: approx 20g (¾oz) or 75cm (30in) of each colour and slightly more of White

• Approx 3.5m (4yd) strong cotton warp thread

• Sharp scissors

• Something to hang the weaving from

• Tapestry, wool or weaving needle (optional)

• Small crochet hook

Adjust amounts of wooltops required according to the size of your loom

To warp up the loom, follow the instructions on page 40

HOW TO MAKE

1. Split the wooltops into pencil-width lengths. If your wooltops break or aren't long enough, just tie them together and hide the knot at the back when you're weaving.

2. Start with three lengths each of Flamingo, Pale Pink and Candy Pink. Knot a fringe along the bottom of the loom in alternate colours as per step 1 on page 41.

3. Fill the row and then repeat with green and white in a new row above. Use alternate warp threads so the knots sit in slightly different places.

4. Trim these knot ends so that the greens sit above the pinks and are even and straight at the base. You can see from the picture that they 'splay' out slightly once they are cut off the loom.

5. Now weave a row of white and then bring in a row of black over the top. Alternate these two colours for another five rows (this is called the 'pick and pick' technique).

6. To make the wooltops tassel heart, see page 43. To weave around the heart, pull a long pencil-width piece of Pale Pink wooltops. Carry the wool behind the heart and come up the other side on each row. Weave 10–12 rows with this, making sure you keep pushing down your work to hide the warp and make it tight. Follow with a few rows of Glittery Unicorn blend.

7. Add two rows of pale blue, but when you weave, pull out little loops of wool for each stitch to give a different textural effect that makes the weave look bigger and stand proud. Follow with 6-7 rows of weaving with Peppermint Green.

8. For a row of 'soumak' weaving, thread the weaving needle with a long length of Bright Yellow. Starting at the right-hand side, take the needle over two warp threads, then backwards over the last one. Keep repeating this all the way across to create a slanted stitch. When you get to the end, reverse this in the opposite direction. This gives a 'plaited' look.

9. Next add ten rows of white, followed by two more rows of 'pulled out' stitches in Flamingo (as step 7).

10. Finally, add five 'pick and pick' rows (as step 5) at the top using Peach and Jade Green.

11. Finish with a line of Candy Pink fringe knots. Trim short enough to see the other colours underneath. Leave a little bit of room at the top of the loom to make it easier to remove the weaving.

12. Carefully slip each end from the loom and if necessary tie off each pair of warp threads. At the base of the weaving, the wooltops knots should hold everything in place.

13. Weave in any loose ends at the back using either the weaving needle or a small crochet hook and hang the weaving from a suitable hanger.

Enchanting the Planting

Catch a falling pot and suspend your foliage from the ceiling in this super easy knotted plant hanger made from wooltops!

WHAT YOU'LL NEED

To make a plant hanger for a pot approx. 24cm (9½in) in diameter. Finished hanger is approx. 110cm (43in) long.

• Wooltops: four 2.2m (7ft) lengths or approx. 250g (9oz) in colour of your choice – I used Hot Pink. Plus smaller lengths for wrapping at top and base – I used under 1m (1yd) of Candy Pink

• Curtain ring or similar (at least 30mm/1¼in diameter)

• A few old bits of yarn (these will be hidden)

• Fabric glue

• Optional: decorative beads, needle and thread, contrasting yarn

HOW TO MAKE

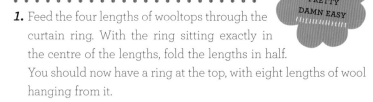

LEVEL
PRETTY
DAMN EASY

1. Feed the four lengths of wooltops through the curtain ring. With the ring sitting exactly in the centre of the lengths, fold the lengths in half. You should now have a ring at the top, with eight lengths of wool hanging from it.

2. If possible, hang the ring up somewhere on the wall or ceiling. This makes things a lot easier! Start by tying a piece of old yarn around the very top to secure all the lengths together.

3. Now wrap your contrasting wooltops around this yarn to hide it. Wrap neatly and tuck in the tails. Secure with a little fabric glue if necessary.

4. Separating the wooltops lengths into pairs, tie a knot in each pair about 30cm (12in) down. Make sure the knots are at the same level for each pair. You should now have four 'lots' of wooltops pairs, each knotted!

5. Now take one piece of wooltops from each adjacent length and knot these together about 15–20cm (6–8in) down, depending on the size of the plant pot to be held inside – one length from one pair, and one length from its neighbouring pair. This will form the 'V' shape. You should still have four 'lots' and four knots.

6. Loosely tie another piece of old yarn about 20cm (8in) further down around the middle. Cover this in contrasting wooltops.

7. You can fray out the bottom of the lengths, or trim them down – it's up to you! Optional: tie a few contrasting pieces of yarn here and there around the base. I used some of my handspun yarns. Add a plant and you're done!

Spinning Stuff with Fluff

Spin your own 'art yarns' from wooltops with a very portable drop spindle. Drop spindle spinning is very different from spinning on a spinning wheel – not quite as fast – but is highly addictive! This is the 'park and draft' method and is the easiest way to get started.

WHAT YOU'LL NEED

• Drop spindle – these come in lots of different shapes and sizes. I used one with a whorl at the top, which is most common and (I find) the easiest to use

• Small piece of 'leader' yarn – about 20cm (8in) is enough and a wool yarn is best; any thickness will do

• Different coloured, blended or hand-dyed wooltops in at least 50cm (20in) lengths or longer

HOW MUCH FLUFF WILL YOU NEED?

100g (3½oz) will spin up 100g of yarn! And so on. However, the 'yardage' or length of the yarn you end up with will depend on the thickness of it as you spin it up.

HOW TO DO IT

1. Start by attaching a 'leader' yarn to your drop spindle. This can be looped across and through or just tied in place around the 'shaft' of the spindle, then it travels up around the 'whorl' (the disc that sticks out) and up again through and around the hook. It will get you off to a good start and gives the fibre something to 'cling to' when you first start spinning.

2. Pull off a manageable length of your chosen wooltops – no more than about 50cm (20in) long. Now split the wooltops into thirds LENGTHWAYS. If you are just using one colour, then prepare a number of pieces to get started. GENTLY and carefully tease out each length of wooltops – but be careful it doesn't get too fine or break.

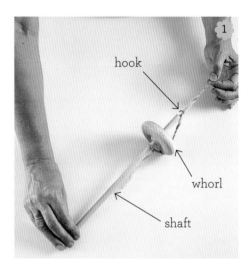

hook

whorl

shaft

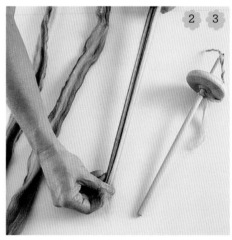

3. Tease one end of it even further. This is called drafting the wool. The thickness of the wool here will determine the thickness of your yarn as you spin! It's so difficult to describe in words – have a go and see how the thickness of the wool affects the outcome.

4. Take the first piece of wooltops that you have lengthened and drafted and overlap one end of it onto the end of the leader yarn, then 'twist it' together between your fingers so that the wooltops surrounds the yarn. Sometimes I dampen my fingers a little as this helps it stick!

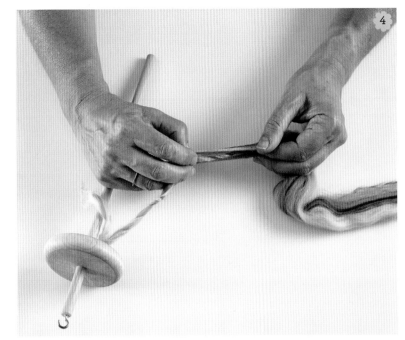

5. If you are right-handed, hold the wooltops in your left hand and the drop spindle in your right hand. It's a good idea to have your left arm horizontal with the wooltops slung across it, so it doesn't interfere with your spinning. If you are left-handed, reverse the whole process!

6. The spindle will be suspended from the wool at the top, which will be hooked around the hook. You will use your right hand to spin the shaft of the spindle from the bottom. I always spin it anti-clockwise – but it's personal preference!

7. Once the wool is attached to the leader yarn and on the shaft of the spindle and through the hook, pinch it with your left forefinger and thumb, about 8–10cm (3–4in) above the hook, to hold the twist before you spin.

8. Suspend the spindle (as step 5) and spin it from the bottom to add energy, which travels up into the wool so it 'spins' into yarn. Take care not to over-spin it so it bunches up in rings.

JOINING BREAKS

If your wooltops breaks off at any point, it's fairly easy to re-join it. Just start from step 1 again and join the new wooltops onto the yarn you've already spun in the same way that we did with the leader yarn at the beginning!

9. Once this piece of wooltops is spun, 'park' the end of the spindle under your left armpit, replace your left forefinger and thumb with your right forefinger and thumb, and draft out your next 8–10cm (3–4in) of wooltops above with your other hand.

10. Release the energy/spin into the new drafted length, but hold it tightly with your finger and thumb above and DO NOT let the twist run into the new wool still to be drafted. If it does, it will make it very difficult to draft.

11. Take the spindle back into your right hand from under your armpit, unhook the yarn from the top hook and WIND it onto the spindle. When the spun yarn is NEARLY all wound on, leave enough spare to re-hook it around the hook several times again for the next session of spinning. Then repeat.

12. Keep repeating this process until you get used to it – draft, spin, draft, spin. You are allowing the energy from the spin to travel into the lengths of wooltops, but you are controlling it by pinching your finger and thumb to stop and start that energy travelling through the wool. **Be careful not to let the spindle spin in the opposite direction, or it will untwist the newly spun yarn and break off!**

13. As you wind on your yarn, keep it even around the top of the spindle just below the whorl. When you can't get any more on there, it's time to wind it off into your first ball of yarn!

14. When you've spun all your wooltops and you're done, wind the yarn into a ball or skein. Optional: wash the yarn in lukewarm water to 'set' the twist. Squeeze the water out gently and leave to dry. It is now ready to use!

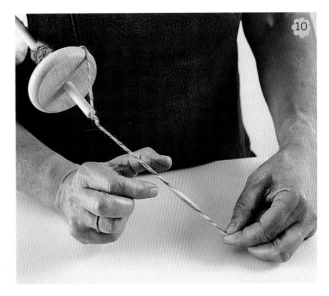

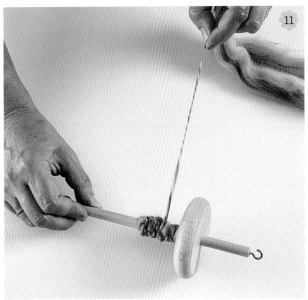

Flufftastic Plastic

Stand out from the crowd by decorating a plastic basket with a fluffy difference. Those punched holes are perfect for threading wool in and out of and this is easy enough for kids to do as well. It's like a giant stitching canvas!

WHAT YOU'LL NEED

• Retro plastic shopping baskets – any size

• Handspun wooltops yarn or shop-bought yarn in lots of different colours

• Tapestry, wool or weaving needle – useful but not essential

• Strong fabric glue

• Pompoms and yarns for decoration

• Buttons and beads for decoration (optional)

I used my own handspun yarn in all the colours of the rainbow, along with plain old wooltops – either whole widths if the holes were big enough, or split up into pencil width lengths and twisted a little to strengthen.

HOW TO MAKE

LEVEL
EASY PEASY

1. Make a plan before you start. Think about the colours that will contrast well against your basket. Look at the holes and decide what sort of design will work.

2. Use a little glue to hold yarn or wool around handles etc. while you wrap or cover them.

3. Weave in the ends and tie off inside the baskets when you're done with each colour. Again, a little glue helps keep things in place if it'll get a lot of use.

FOR THE PINK BASKET Take various colours of wooltops and tie them randomly around different parts of the basket with a double knot at the front. Trim to allow the wooltops to splay out into little bow shapes. Bind off the handles using some yarn, carefully wrapping the yarn around. I used a mixture of Fluorescent Orange and handspun Glittery Unicorn blend. Add some yarn and wooltops pompoms to decorate at each side (see page 8).

FOR THE TURQUOISE BASKET For this basket I decided to keep it simple with vertical stripes in lots of different colours. I used handspun yarn for this and wove it in and out of the holes according to how long the lengths were.

FOR THE YELLOW BASKET Here I wound some handspun Knit Collage Gypsy Garden yarn around the handles, and then decorated up the sides with the same yarn mixed with my own handspun yarn. I added a large pink flower bead in the centre.

TOP TIP

Add a fabric liner into your basket to protect your designs from getting rubbed against too much.

Highly Strung

Make your own stylish lampshades in colours to suit your room! Either spin up some unique yarn on a drop spindle or use a shop-bought yarn.

WHAT YOU'LL NEED

• Lampshade frame – I used a 20 x 20cm (8 x 8in) frame

• Enough yarn to wrap around the frame – I used approx. 60g (2oz)

• Tapestry, wool or weaving needle

• Strong glue

• Extra matching wooltops or yarn to make pompoms (optional)

See page 54 for spinning instructions to make your own yarn

LEVEL
EASY PEASY

TOP TIP

Recycle an old lampshade if you don't want to buy a new one!

HOW TO MAKE

1. Start by winding your yarn into a ball small enough to pass through the centre of the shade.

2. Tie off the yarn onto the frame at the top, leaving about a 5cm (2in) tail.

3. Wind the yarn around the frame from top to bottom as tightly as you can without breaking it.

4. The closer you 'string' up the shade, the less light will shine through and the more yarn you'll need. You can see from the picture that I've left quite a few gaps. This creates pretty patterns on the wall when the light is switched on!

5. When you've completed the winding, tie off the yarn to the tail you left at the beginning. Trim the ends (weave these in on the inside once you've finished).

6. Thread a long length of remaining yarn through a weaving needle and sew the yarn around the frame at the top and the bottom, to hide any of the white parts still showing.

7. Bunch up the yarn around the uprights to hide these too and dab a little spot of glue to hold in place.

8. Decide which way up your lampshade will be used, then make six little pompoms (see page 8). Leave a 10cm (4in) tail on each one, and tie them on tight at the base of each upright.

JOINING BREAKS

If you are using a handspun yarn it may be a little more delicate than a shop-bought yarn. If it does break while stringing the shade, then just tie it back together and carry on. No one will notice!

LEVEL
EASY PEASY

Basket Case

Pimp up a straw or wicker basket with a unique makeover. All you need are a few pieces of wooltops, handspun or shop-bought yarn – and some fluffy pompoms!

WHAT YOU'LL NEED

• Straw or wicker basket

• Handspun wooltops yarn or shop-bought yarn in lots of different colours – I used my own handspun yarn in: Bright Yellow, Flamingo, Jade, Cornflower, Candy, Grass Green, Turquoise, Glittery Unicorn and Lilac

• Tapestry, wool or weaving needle

• Strong fabric glue

• Wooltops pompoms (see page 8)

TOP TIP

Try this method on other things too! Add some of these little handspun yarn knots onto open weave fabrics or cushions too. It's a really quick and effective way to decorate things.

HOW TO MAKE

1. Using shortish pieces of yarn about 20cm (8in) long, thread up your weaving needle.

2. Carefully pass it under one of the pieces of straw in your basket, release the needle and tie a double knot.

3. Trim the ends and your first little knot is made. It's as simple as that! If you are using handspun wooltops, then the end of each little knot will splay out nicely.

4. Now repeat these little knots all over your basket quite randomly here and there in different colours.

5. When you are done, add a tiny spot of fabric glue into the centre of each knot and leave to dry. This will make sure they stay put!

6. Make a couple of matching pompoms (I used Glittery Unicorn wooltops for this) and leave a long tail on each to hang down from one of the handles.

The Holey Trinity Cushion

This cushion uses the same fluffy wooltops in three different ways! First handspun and then knitted into the cushion front, then wet felted for the back and finally used for pompoms to adorn each corner.

WHAT YOU'LL NEED

For a 30cm (12in) square cushion

• 150g (5½oz) wooltops – I used hand-dyed Malabrigo Nube in colour Diana
• Drop spindle
• One pair of 6.5mm (US 10½) knitting needles
• Spray bottle, iron and tea towel
• Bamboo mat, net, soap and water (for wet felting)
• Pins, needle and thread
• Pompom maker
• Sharp scissors and matching embroidery cotton
• Button (optional)
• Toy stuffing or cushion pad

HOW TO MAKE

1. Hand spin 50g (1¾oz) of the wooltops (see page 54) and wind into a ball.

2. Using the 6.5mm knitting needles and handspun yarn, cast on 36 stitches.

3. Knit one row. Purl one row. Repeat these two rows until the piece is square. Cast (bind) off. Pin flat to an ironing board or similar. Spray with a fine mist of water. Place a tea towel over the top and iron gently on a low heat. Leave to dry in desired shape.

4. Using the next 50g (1¾oz) of wooltops, make a piece of flat felt (see page 22). Your piece of felt should be approx. 20% longer than the cushion front when it's finished, and slightly wider in all directions for sewing together. Leave to dry.

5. Cut the felt in half widthways and overlap the centre to match the length of the knitted front . Expose the beautiful 'finished' frilly edge of the felt on the outside of the overlap if you can!

6. With right sides facing, pin, then hand sew the knitted front and two felt pieces together around the edge. Turn right side out through the envelope opening.

7. Optional: add a button onto the underneath flap of felt and cut a buttonhole in the top flap to fasten. The felt won't fray, but don't cut the buttonhole too large – keep it fairly snug!

8. Make four pompoms (see page 8) from the remaining wooltops. Use strong embroidery cotton to tie and then sew the pompoms onto each corner of the cushion, hiding the finishing knots on the inside of the cover. Stuff with a cushion pad or stuffing.

TOP TIP

If your drop spindle spinning has produced a thicker yarn, then choose larger needles to knit with – you might have ended up with less yarn in length, but the larger needles will make it go further! Likewise, if your handspun yarn is very fine, choose a smaller sized needle so the cushion front will have a closer knit.

Cushty Cushion

A quick knit using wooltops. Make this giant knitted cushion for your sofa in no time!

WHAT YOU'LL NEED

For a cushion approx. 65cm (26in) square

• 1.75kg (approx. 4lb) wooltops – I used undyed White

• One pair of 30mm (1¼in) giant knitting needles, at least 50cm (20in) long

• Small pieces of coloured felt for the flowers – I used homemade (see page 22) but you can also use readymade

• Matching embroidery cotton

• Tapestry, wool or weaving needle

• Pins, needle and thread

• Beads or buttons to sit in the middle of the flowers, in contrasting colours

• Readymade felt for the back (slightly larger than the finished knitted front)

• Sharp scissors

• Button (optional)

• Cushion pad

LEVEL
EASY ONCE YOU KNOW HOW

HOW TO MAKE

1. Using the 30mm knitting needles and the wooltops, cast on 15 stitches. Knit one row. Purl one row. Repeat these two rows until the piece is square. Cast (bind) off and weave in wispy ends of wooltops to hide them.

2. Cut 10 little felt flowers and leaves in different colours (see page 36) and sew each one into place randomly dotted around the cushion front using the embroidery thread and needle. Sew through the bead or button on top as you sew it all together. Hide the knots at the back of the cushion front.

3. Cut two pieces of white felt for the back of the cushion that are very slightly wider than your knitting and about 20cm (8in) longer than the cushion size.

4. Lay them on top of one another, overlapping the centre to match the length of the knitted front.

5. With right sides facing, pin, then hand sew the knitted front and two felt pieces together around the edge. Turn right side out through the envelope opening.

6. Optional: add a button onto the underneath flap of felt and cut a buttonhole to fasten. The felt won't fray, but don't cut the buttonhole too large – keep it fairly snug!

7. Stuff with a cushion pad.

TO CONCEAL 'JOINS'

Overlap the two wispy ends of wooltops you need to join by about 15cm (6in), and use an old piece of regular yarn to loosely tie it together. Knit with it as normal, and then a couple of rows later carefully snip the yarn you used to tie it together and remove. It will be seamlessly 'joined' and no one will ever know!

Stole Goals

Knit this stylish warm stole in less than an hour using wooltops. It's a great alternative to a fur stole and is super warm!

WHAT YOU'LL NEED

For a stole approx. 130cm (51in) x 25cm (10in)

• 800g (28oz) wooltops in the colour of your choice – I used Grey

• One pair of 30mm (1¼in) giant knitting needles, at least 50cm (20in) long

• Spray bottle, iron and tea towel

• Optional: Watercolour Corsage to fasten (see page 36)

HOW TO MAKE

1. Using the 30mm knitting needles and the wooltops, cast on 5 stitches. Knit one row. Purl one row. Repeat these two rows to the desired length. Cast (bind) off and weave in wispy ends of wooltops to hide them.

2. Pin flat to an ironing board or similar. Spray with a fine mist of water. Place a tea towel over the stole and iron gently on a low heat. Leave to dry in the desired shape.

3. Wear the stole on your shoulders as opposed to around your neck. It can be stylishly fixed in the middle with a corsage or brooch to hold it in place.

TOP TIP

Keep your knitting as LOOSE as possible, making sure you pull plenty of wooltops through for each stitch. Really keep this in mind as you are making. It feels quite different from knitting with regular fine yarn, and is of course much faster!

Rows for Toes

This super-easy crochet rug is so fast to make – and what could be cosier underfoot than fluffy wooltops?

WHAT YOU'LL NEED

For a rug approx. 80cm (32in) in diameter – excluding pompoms!

• Wooltops – I used 1.7kg (3¾lb) Angel's Delight blend (main colour) and 500g (1lb) Lettuce Green (edging)

• 22–25mm (⅞–1in) giant crochet hook

• 11 Wooltops Pompoms (see page 8) – I used Pale Yellow Olive

• Felt flower and leaves for centre (see page 36)

• Matching embroidery cotton

• Tapestry, wool or weaving needle

TOP TIP

Keep an eye on the rug as you are crocheting as your wooltops – and therefore your tension (gauge) – may be slightly different from mine. If the rug starts to cup upwards, then add a few more stitches into your round. If it cups downwards, then decrease a few stitches. The aim is to keep it as flat as possible.

HOW TO MAKE

1. Using the crochet hook and main colour wooltops, make 5 chains and then slip stitch into the first chain to make a ring. You will now work around the ring using double crochet (dc) stitches (US single crochet).

Rounds 1–2: Work 2 dc into each chain or stitch.

Round 3: Work 1 dc and 2 dc into alternate stitches.

Rounds 4–7: Work 1 dc into each of the first 2 stitches, then 2 dc into the next stitch all the way around.

2. Change to the edging colour and add another 1 or 2 rounds, working 1 dc into each stitch.

3. Finish by making a slip stitch into the first stitch of the last round. Fasten off and weave in the ends on the underside of the rug.

4. Sew a small flower and two leaves securely to the centre.

5. Sew or tie each pompom in place so that they are equidistant around the outside of the rug.

LEVEL
EASY ONCE
YOU KNOW HOW

Granny Bounce

Your Granny will actually bounce when she jumps out of bed and lands on this giant granny square rug. Make it in no time using wooltops and a giant hook...

WHAT YOU'LL NEED

For a rug approx. 112cm (44in) 'square'

• Wooltops – I used 400g (14oz) Pale Pink, 700g (25oz) Salmon Pink, 900g (32oz) Burgundy, 350g (12oz) Flamingo, 450g (16oz) Light Turquoise, 950g (33½oz) Lettuce Green and 650g (23oz) Bright Yellow

• 22–25mm (⅞–1in) giant crochet hook

• Wooltops pompoms (see page 8) for centre (optional) – I used Bright Red and Bright Yellow

HOW TO MAKE

1. Using the crochet hook and Pale Pink wooltops, make 6 chains and then slip stitch into the first chain to make a ring. You will now work around the ring using treble crochet (tr) stitches (US double crochet).

Round 1: Make 3 chains (counts as first tr), work 2 tr into the ring, 3 chains (corner space), *3 tr into the ring, 3 chains; repeat from * twice more, then join with slip stitch into top of beginning 3 chains. Fasten off.

2. Join Salmon Pink to any corner space of round 1.

Round 2: Make 3 chains (counts as first tr), work 2 tr into corner space, 3 chains, 3 tr into same corner space, 1 chain, *(3 tr, 3 chains, 3 tr) into next corner space, 1 chain; repeat from * twice more, then join with slip stitch into top of beginning 3 chains. Fasten off. Note that each 3 chains of this round forms a new corner space and each 1 chain forms a side space.

3. Join Burgundy to any corner space of round 2.

Round 3: Starting with 3 chains to count as the first tr, work around the square making (3 tr, 2 chains, 3 tr) in each corner space and 3 tr in each side space, then join with slip stitch into top of beginning 3 chains. Fasten off.

4. You will now work around the rug using double crochet (dc) stitches (US single crochet).

Round 4: Change to Flamingo and work 1 dc into each chain or stitch.

Round 5: Change to Light Turquoise and work 1 dc into each stitch.

Rounds 6–7: Change to Lettuce Green and work 1 dc into each stitch but add an extra 1 dc roughly at each corner point on both rounds to help it lay flatter.

Round 8: Change to Bright Yellow, *make 3 chains, slip stitch into each of the next 4 stitches of round 7; repeat from * all around, then join with slip stitch into first chain made. Fasten off.

5. Weave in the ends on the underside of the rug.

6. Tie the pompoms in place in the centre of the rug to finish.

Potted and Knotted

Crochet this plant pot cover in less than an hour using a giant crochet hook and wooltops as your yarn. Optional felt flowers add decoration to the front when it's finished.

WHAT YOU'LL NEED

For a pot approx. 22cm (9in) in diameter by 22cm (9in) high

LEVEL

PRETTY DAMN EASY

- 700g (25oz) wooltops – I used Light Turquoise
- 22–25mm (⅞–1in) giant crochet hook
- Felt flowers and leaves to decorate (see page 36)

HOW TO MAKE

1. Using the crochet hook and wooltops, make 5 chains and then slip stitch into the first chain to make a ring. You will now work around the ring using double crochet (dc) stitches (US single crochet).

2. **Round 1:** Work 2 dc into each chain.

3. **Round 2:** Work 1 dc into each stitch.

4. **Round 3:** Work 1 dc into the back loop only of each stitch (this will form the edge of the base).

5. You will now crochet upwards for the sides by working 1 dc into each stitch around and around until you reach the desired height. Finish in line with where you started working up the sides so that you complete a full final round for a neater edge.

6. Fasten off and weave in the ends on the inside of the pot cover.

7. Add felt flowers and leaves to decorate.

CARING FOR KNITTED AND CROCHETED WOOLTOPS PROJECTS

The wooltops are strong once crocheted or knitted together, and the tighter it is, the less it will pill and shed. However, some pilling and shedding will always take place with any fine wool. This is normal. If you treat it carefully, however, it should last and look good. Never wash these items – dry clean only.

Dyeing Wooltops & Yarns

It's easier to dye wool yarns, fibres and wooltops than you might imagine! The process is simple. A pre-soaking of the fibres with some citric acid, followed by a blast of heat, will result in dyes that are fixed to your wool, with amazing results depending on how you mix and apply the dyes.

Enjoy experimenting with colours and applications. Different application techniques give very different results! 'Paint' the dyes on with a brush, drip them on from a bottle, liberally pour them on, or you can even sprinkle on the dry powder in small amounts for speckle effects. As long as you are careful to exhaust the dye and make sure it's fixed correctly, your results should be light-fast and wash-fast.

Before you start it's important to realise that the finished results will depend on lots of different elements: the amount of dye you use, the acidity of your dye bath, and the quantity of wool you have in relation to the liquid. Trial and error is the only way to fully understand how these different components will fully affect the outcome!

BEFORE YOU START

Safety is key. You will need goggles and a face mask and rubber gloves. And you need to use them! Don't risk your health and safety for some dyed wool. It's not worth it!

- Don't dye near food prep areas.

- Use a separate set of pans, bottles and spoons etc. that are NOT used for food.

- Use a separate microwave or pot or steamer that isn't used for food (pick up a microwave cheaply secondhand if you get hooked).

- Don't eat while you are dyeing – keep your rubber gloves on.

- Wash everything thoroughly when you're done – especially your hands.

WHAT YOU'LL NEED

To dye 400g (appox. 1lb) of wooltops or yarn

• Goggles, face mask, rubber gloves and apron

• Bucket for pre-soaking

• 1 tbsp citric acid

• Sealable squirty bottles, jugs and spoons

• Acid dyes in a range of colours

• Clingfilm

• Old microwave or a large pot for the stove

• Salt (optional)

• Measuring jug and measuring spoon

• Access to a sink and hot and cold water, and a protected work surface

TOP TIP

Keep notes about how you dyed your test pieces and label them when you're done. This is truly invaluable information later on when you love the results but can't remember what you did!

HOW TO DO IT

1. Make sure your wool is clean so nothing prevents the dyes from working. Fill a bucket with enough lukewarm water to cover the wooltops or yarn.

2. I prefer to use citric acid with my dyes rather than vinegar, as it doesn't smell, and is easily available. Dissolve 1 tbsp citric acid into this water per 400g of wool.

3. Leave the wooltops or yarn to soak for at least an hour in this solution (longer or overnight if you can).

4. Make up your dyes. It's useful to have some small sealable squirty bottles for this so you can store unused dye. It's up to you how concentrated you make the dye solutions. Less dye will give more pastel effects. More will result in deeper colour. Start with 1 tsp of dye powder diluted with a few drops of boiling water and then add 200ml (7fl oz) of warm water once dissolved.

5. Wring out your wooltops or yarn gently. If you are using the microwave method, lay out some clingfilm onto a protected surface and lay the wooltops on top. Apply your dye(s) with whichever method you choose.

6. Microwave method: wrap the wooltops or yarn up carefully in the clingfilm and pop it into the microwave. Microwave on 50–75% power for about 2 minutes depending on the power settings of your microwave. Stove top method : immerse wool into a pan of cold water and bring to just below boiling, stirring occasionally, for 30–60 minutes. A spoonful of salt in the pot can help to exhaust the dye.

7. Leave the wooltops or yarn to cool FULLY before touching or rinsing. Agitating the fibres whilst they are still hot will start to felt the wool – this is the biggest risk with wooltops. It needs to be treated very gently!

8. Once cooled, rinse thoroughly under cool water to remove excess dye. In an ideal scenario, not too much excess dye will run out. This means the dye has been exhausted and taken up by the wool. If the dye doesn't exhaust well, try a slightly more powerful setting or longer in the microwave or on the stove top. Or try using slightly more citric acid or less dye.

9. Once the water runs clear, leave the wooltops or yarn to dry naturally. Then it's ready to use.

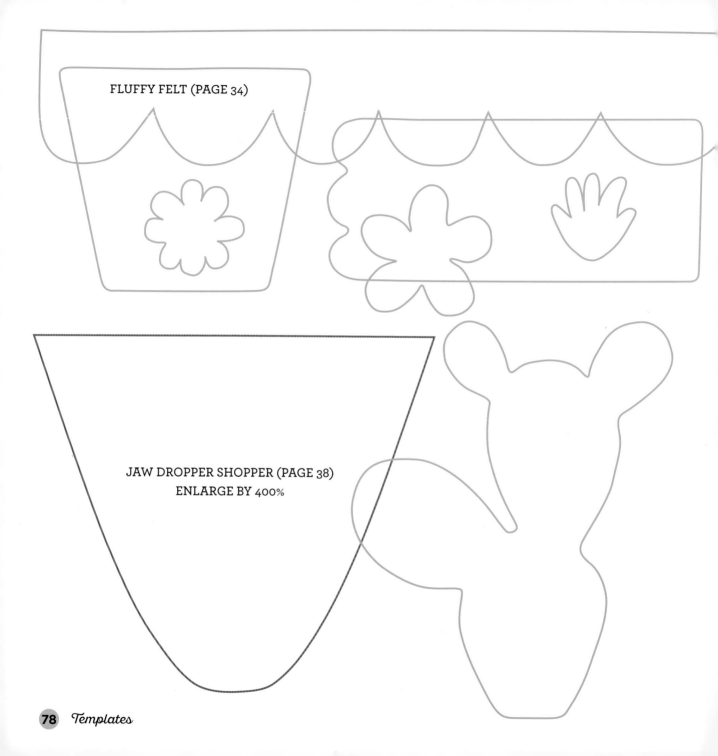

FLUFFY FELT (PAGE 34)

JAW DROPPER SHOPPER (PAGE 38)
ENLARGE BY 400%

Resources

Everything you need to make the projects
in this book is available online at:

www.gilliangladrag.co.uk

(we ship worldwide) or from our shop:

The Gilliangladrag Fluff-a-torium
20 West Street
Dorking
Surrey
RH4 1BL
UK

ONLINE TUTORIALS

Check out Gillian's YouTube channel for free
videos about the basics of felting: there are
free tutorials on needle felting, flat wet felting
and 3D felting.

Photography by Rachel Whiting

First published in the United Kingdom in 2017 by
Pavilion
43 Great Ormond Street
London
WC1N 3HZ

Copyright © Pavilion Books Company Ltd 2017
Text © Gillian Harris 2017

Distributed in the United States and Canada by
Sterling Publishing Co., Inc. 1166 Avenue of the Americas,
New York, NY 10036

ISBN 978-1-911216-19-3

A CIP catalogue record for this book is available from the
British Library.

10 9 8 7 6 5 4 3 2 1

Repro by Colourdepth, UK
Printed and bound by 1010 Printing International Ltd, China

This book can be ordered direct from the publisher at
www.pavilionbooks.com